WHEN HOLLYWOOD COMES TO YOU

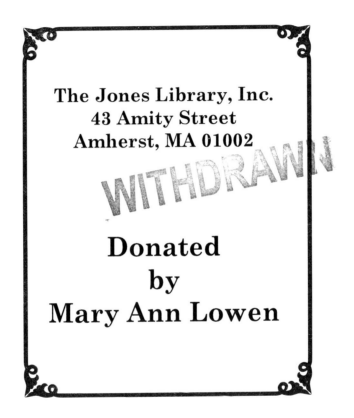

WHEN HOLLYWOOD COMES TO YOU

VINCENT GUERRA

Four Way Books
Tribeca

Please direct all inquiries to:
Editorial Office
Four Way Books
POB 535, Village Station
New York, NY 10014
www.fourwaybooks.com

Library of Congress Cataloging-in-Publication Data

Names: Guerra, Vincent, 1983- author.
Title: When Hollywood comes to you / Vincent Guerra.
Description: New York, NY : Four Way Books, 2017.
Identifiers: LCCN 2017000679 | ISBN 9781945588037 (pbk. : alk. paper)
Classification: LCC PS3607.U462 A6 2017 | DDC 811/.6--dc23
LC record available at https://lccn.loc.gov/2017000679

This book is manufactured in the United States of America and printed on acid-free paper.

Four Way Books is a not-for-profit literary press. We are grateful for the assistance
we receive from individual donors, public arts agencies, and private foundations.

This publication is made possible with public funds from the National Endowment for the Arts

and with public funds from the New York State Council on the Arts,
a state agency.

We are a proud member of the Community of Literary Magazines and Presses.

Distributed by University Press of New England
One Court Street, Lebanon, NH 03766

for Carol and Phil and Ann
and Rachel and Stephanie and Anthony

Contents

Lost in the Trinket Machines

The Roy Orbison Inside Us All 3
The Stir of Your Avoided Life 4
The Television Detective's Red Hair 6
Sardine Lake, 1992 7
Carnival Light 11
To the Shopping Mall 13
Lost in the Trinket Machines 14
Drive 16
On the Yo-Yo 18

No Class Enjoyments

No Class Enjoyments 23
Morning Will Be Without Cruelty from Now On 25
Robert Walser and Cheeseburger 26
Some Similarities Between Dogs and Children 28
For Christ's Sake, Pay Attention 30
Mobile Tanning Unit 32
Outlook Crooning 34
And Why Not Just Kamikaze 36
Something's Coming Soon 37
The Year I Finally Fake My Death 39

Dead Man

New Year's with Reactive Arthritis   43
The Manatees   47
Am I Paralyzed?   49
Discarded Cosmos   51
Haberdashery   53
Rewrite   55
Dead Man   58

Lost in the Trinket Machines

The Roy Orbison Inside Us All

Some of us live immured in the junior high of our minds. Among the embryos of adult desires. In that bedroom marked with caution tape, closed off to parents, to our workday lives, we press repeat on our favorite song. We press repeat again. And our life fades out. Like nocturnal animals, our feelings only come out at night, just there to tear into us a bit. It's not the type of mourning that comes with a police escort and a placard for your dash. It's your life. It keeps going. Here's a Kleenex. In each of us there's a loneliness wearing prescription sunglasses. In each, there's the march of Roy's guitar, lilac faint and mounting. And Roy is proof that beauty comes from ugliness: Roy's from Texas. Maybe the lonely oil fields await us. Maybe that picked-over yard has one more morsel for a boy. And maybe if we do try our engine, we'll flood it. Listen, we can sit shotgun in someone else's anxious dream. We've done it before. Maybe Roy's no Elvis, but there's room for us in his Cadillac, where even the weird-looking roar with confidence. And lord knows we're weird looking.

THE STIR OF YOUR AVOIDED LIFE

You didn't wake
in dewy blue bitter

panic or prairie
june or spangle grass—

no field, no shopping-
cart encampment

of tarpaulin and toddler's
clothes—though wet-

eyed,
though whelmed

in bottled-
up a.m. light, your

lungs confined like tidal
anemone or beds

of strawberries tucked
in their black plastic

sheeting. You can
get used to almost

anything—strip mall
flowers for startle, a sitcom

for cloister—you
can go entire

days without feeling
anything at all.

No one's your
rouser, no one

your awful salts;
calm is

an alarm in a beige
waiting room—is you,

the alarm.

THE TELEVISION DETECTIVE'S RED HAIR

Is carnival light. Is morning's worn out arrival
for the victim's parents. Is coffee in a Styrofoam
cup and packets of sweetener the pink and blue
of baby's clothes. Is an abalone glow in a little
brother's bedroom window. First, the bad news.
After walking a wide row in a wet field poking
the soil. Is the loss that brings the weather on.
That boxes up belongings. In the drone of the
day. In the din and double-talk. Doldrums of
work and feeling useless. Something resurfaces
in us. A partial print. A partial plate. And her
voice as plain and sure as a Texas porch. The
taciturn of sacred. Waiting alone in a dreary
car. In the orange light outside the suspect's
apartment. You have the right to remain as you
are. Or pursue that noise. Through the cracked
door of the pines. That strain in the lake's dis-
tortion. Song massaging the feeling back in.
What is worth our devotion. What charges
us. A charmed sequence of words. The jangle.
The strum. Truth and beauty. And what have
I done with my life. Is the sheer of decision.
Is the from here on out. Is one's own thought.
One's own moment. This is the good news.

Sardine Lake, 1992

My father wandered and found them
        rose quartz, amethyst, obsidian

a dandelion's ghosted globe

and a stupid paper chart
for lost alone in the woods

in our sarcophagi sleeping bags
and our arms in our shirts

        each starry animal
the major and minor

and the glacier's pale belly
upon the rocks

in the tilted valley where we camped

my brother, younger, unknowing
this will end

My father held the flashlight

crowded by pines, his bristled face
his smell

I knew then I didn't care
about stars
        but what was close

wouldn't last

      *

Swings and graveyards
        double-shifts

never feeling quite himself

his clay torso in the shed
beneath a sheet of plastic

life piled on life

For what?—

the thoughts
that sometimes come

we don't write down

The years commuted

in his silver Tercel with half a million miles
the melatonin, felt curtains

earplugs in order
to sleep through the day

       *

In the monochrome
       of the macula, the either/or
of the eye

the Sierras under sheets
of snow, an unused room

I sat awake in

a rehearsal of birds
Venus

indian paintbrush mixing its pigments
till my eyes adjust

And in the morning we'd switchback
toward the lookout

the metal stairway like a carnival ride
       in which the ride is
        standing and looking

across airy mountains

where one can see from miles
the fires

We gnashed our jerky
       and on the sunny metal

slipped off our packs

seemed to float

CARNIVAL LIGHT

Cuff me
in florescence. Let me
Fly Away. Let

me Kamikaze. But everything's
expensive. And every child
captive of every

midway caller. My eyes
are barkers. My
runaway strut

through spangled darkness
slips past squads
of idolic adolescents—my arms

into my pockets—donning neon-glo
bracelets. Lock me up
in a soaring mechanism. I flee

into the calm
among the animals. Quiet fireworks
of impulse. Familiar music. My body

the perfect dark
on which each explosion's flowering
can be felt. On which each

fades out. The hundred
silhouetted starlets.
A Coke with ice

in a red paper cup. Why return
to this fugitive palace. The pines
are still—immense

and silent.
The end of summer
sweetens the needles.

To the Shopping Mall

This is what I'm asked to love. Of course
the sun is white and hot and indifferent.
It is saying, I present you, again, with this
unsparkling pavement. I wanted a pair
of shoes for all occasions and weathers.
I hiked along the road without a side-
walk and hunched under the boughs
that required my hunching. I didn't care
if others saw me hunch below the low
branches, passing in their tinted cars.
The world was made for them. I saw a
woman approach from afar in a yellow
dress, who I thought was my reward, but
she too passed me as if she didn't know
me, which she didn't. Everything seemed
figured out, or, if not figured out, hope-
lessly confused. I wanted to ride a good
mood until it broke only at the end of
me, along my most uninhabited shore.
Only then did I want to be touched. I
could feel the cold air coming from the
north. Soon the sun would go, and there
would be mosquitoes. The air cluttered
with tiny wings. It sounds almost nice
put in those words. Tiny wings to lift the
blood.

LOST IN THE TRINKET MACHINES

That a child's
    pink blow-up guitar, something
  so worthless, exists at all,
that feeling migrating
  to nearly everything around you—the sign
  for a mattress sale, the planetary
    names of cars, the desultory layout
of your hometown—making you hateful. Frank says,
    "It's more important to affirm
  even the least sincere." I wish I were
    more like you, Frank. I have no fun
  at county fairs. The animals
depress me. The stuffed
  animals depress me. The contests
where it seems like only Ms. Jacob's fifth-grade class
    entered and won it all. Isn't that life—
    the narcissists always win
  because the narcissists always enter? Meanwhile,
the unofficial beauties prolong
  and proliferate in darkness like rare
  mushrooms, likely never consumed. Does it
make them more
    beautiful that they arrive and pass away
    without a printed ribbon or glass encasement?
I had spent my grandmother's money

on a Smurf key chain in the midway. She
exchanged twenty dollars for a handful
of tokens. When I spent those
tokens in the trinket machines, she purchased
more. I remember her little yellow car
climbing the hill. I remember waiting
on the porch for it. I have participated
in a series of anticipations since
my birth, each with its own measure
of worry. Each with its own
power of imbuing worth. But now
I'm going to take my attention away.

DRIVE

Borrow the car and go some-
where clean. In throbbing dark
the windshield stars distill
themselves, become invisible
by a girl touching the light to
check her makeup. Close your
eyes and blur the mile markers.
Goodbye, lunar walls. Goodbye,
ceiling stars. What is the world
made of when gravity abandons
us. What is the warm air when
I close my eyes. Surround me
again. And what do I deserve.
To eat at a table like a person.
To be spoken to like a person.
A lavender house, new blue-
jean lap, detergent of a girl's
shirt. The stars smudge out in
the cloud cover. How long until
we suffocate. How long before
we tire of our lips. The radio is
a pulsar across the forest roads.
Goodbye, celestial graveyard.
What do I owe. Tell me what I

owe. And know, as you kill the
engine in the dark drive, some-
one has waited in the blue light
for you to come home.

ON THE YO-YO

It is her job to test your harness,
to lift you above midway

drifters and disaffected children,
clutching dashboard dice, a flush hand

of red paper tickets. Yes, you know
it's fixed. But in the pixilated dark,

she says, "Scream," and you tender
your dying scream. And asks,

"Have you had enough?" But no angels defect.
Tennis shoes' glitter paint

like glass, foal legs in jean shorts
before each carriage morphs

into pumpkin or rat. Tonight, marionette,
a mechanical hand will harness

your candescent flesh; faintly each
of the hundred tinted bulbs,

each lucent tulip spots you
among the wings of mournful dusk,

pine, and brown house moths,
trembling aloft the crowded drag

of airbrushed trailers and corn dog stands,
sea foam porta-potties and carts with flavored ice,

extension cords criss-crossing the trampled grass.
Above the crush,

in orbit, in adorned thoughts of,
Remember these three minutes

in my every molecule, she presses
the stop and releases you

across the corrugated floor, loud
with your old gravity.

No Class Enjoyments

No Class Enjoyments

There are deer trails along the road that are not deer trails but person trails, with bits of green glass embedded, where the carless walk to work or walk all day. Here, I pass a white woman, in peach jogging top, who tells me with her smile that she is not distressed, fully conscious of her on-the-street-ness, gulping down the day, never fully quaffed of such a day.

She is enjoying the day like the British Romantic poets enjoyed the day. She is carrying on a tradition that only she and them—Wordsworth, Keats, and her—have sensed within themselves: the divinity of the world. And it is such a shame that others do not feel so much, that others simply cannot enjoy the day—and life!—to the extreme that she, at this street corner, waiting to cross, now enjoys it. I think she may, in fact, *be* British.

I didn't tell her that I, too, enjoy the day and that all the ocean's refuse and animal froth I used to fear as a child—the whips of seaweed, abandoned bodies of crustaceans—I don't fear anymore, that I walk among the highway rubble—the honeycombs of windshield glass, shreds of rubber, a fast food wrapper's flattened wings— along the roar of the shore: these are reason enough to feel calm and cheerful.

MORNING WILL BE WITHOUT CRUELTY FROM NOW ON

My mouth is stuffed with banana slices—
am I a child again? I will be like the dragonflies
in the parking lot, unknowing, as if aloft
in a primordial meadow. Inside my nostrils,
entire skies, entire heavens. Perhaps I am annoying
to these women. If I forget myself, if I lose
myself intentionally, I'll find my doggy way.
My proper place is at my feet. Someday all
of our knees will be wrapped in bandages.
And I can carry nearly everything in the pockets
of my pants. I am a freighter, a cargo boat,
my lower half. And, above, I am bright
sails, crested, a ship's hand in the crow's nest.
Will she be pleased by the pattern of my wings?
Or shall I lie in the street like a plastic bag, my limbs
tumbling and folding in the flattening wind.

Robert Walser and Cheeseburger

The homeless man looks more alive today. He wears his hair in a ponytail beneath a sailor's hat. He is vibrant but too thin to be a sailor. I have never really taken advantage of my looks.

I myself am tired of the same routine of tree and sky and lake. Tired of the same imprisoned faces. Finally, the small man leaves. Finally, he goes home to his minuscule children. He looks like a dumber Ron Howard, if that's possible. I've noticed that many people here have disproportionately large heads.

And the man walking up the stairs is dying very slowly. But, perhaps, he is dying faster than I am dying, sitting here watching him. It's getting darker, which is my preference. The dying man has a sweet smile and a large, sweaty stomach.

I will not use my dog to impress women. I will impress women with my own doggy faithfulness. And now a woman arrives who reminds me of Caroline. She is a picture of equanimity, and, already, I feel demeaned. I feel scrawled on a prison wall. A desperate and worshipped scrawl. I would lower myself so far for this young woman. How far, we have yet to see. But the feeling is far. My feeling is very far. I will wait for her like certain animals wait.

It has taken the dying man one and one half hours to eat his cheeseburger.

I've decided that I would like to meet a woman who

at some point in her life has won a foot race. Step forward, all you champions.

And yesterday, my feet were so cold they felt broken. I wrapped them in a wool blanket till they stung with cold fire. I felt like a child. But there was little I could do. No warm bath. No woman's voice. Just this memory of being four that kept appearing in me. I wore a red shirt, I think. A broken bottle, I knew, was there. A basketball court. A bicycle.

For once I'd like to be gentle with myself. I will touch the trees as I pass. It's okay to touch things like trees. And to walk without purpose. I know soon the sun will not be as kind.

SOME SIMILARITIES BETWEEN DOGS AND CHILDREN

Dogs and children stare—they
are allowed. Dogs wait
outside like children.
They wait in the car
trying to keep upbeat. They lift
their heads for love, for
their happy bodies
to be touched again. Some dogs
have haircuts from the 1980s.
Some dogs are always
smiling, like Jan
from work. A dog knows
how not to press, not to live a life
he doesn't really want. This dog
smiles and shivers
in the shadowed doorway, the profile
of his head, a monument. In glass bricks
that kaleidoscope the street, he
is myriad. How
do we account
for the constant suffering
and agitation of dogs?
Their chemistry
at birth, or their submission?
But we, too,
find ourselves suddenly

abandoned and feel
like lying down again
in the sun-warm street.

FOR CHRIST'S SAKE, PAY ATTENTION

Keep up, Imagination, you bore.
Outside light, you know, is often
quivering, and sometimes presents
a rhombus full of quiver on the
floor. Sometimes, you yourself are
quiverful and would be a light blue
wall with the shadow of bamboo
upon it, like the light of a sister's
crystal dangling in her window.
And inside this rhombus, the air
is full of myriad floating particles.
A double helix kite twirling to the
ceiling. I am not taking in a kind
of nothing air, but an air popu-
lated by small structural models,
turning and glimmering in my
patience. Fireflies passing in and
out of the light, they rise with my
breath and the pressure systems
of my small apartment. They are
mathematical, like mouthwash
or shampoo commercials, viewed
this close. My own hand becomes
a foreign country. Finally, I am

entirely unknown! My real body
is hairier than my imagined body.
And what lovely fingernail sheen,
paneled like a station wagon.

Mobile Tanning Unit

I wanted one of those hot
muffins,

guns or religion,

where women in salmon blouses
buy one get one free.

Hints of genitals
make life seem one big remember
my genitals. A white couple

in denim. The skin
peels away from the madrones.

They loaded 24-packs of soda
onto the long boat. And crossed,

the car-glittered lot like something
Grecian.

I wanted a single shot, a tall, small
wake-up bomb. A muffin to level

a hunger. A rapture. A pick-me-up.
To let go

in a pose of surrender, like a bather
on Bikini Beach, when

Hollywood Comes to You—

let the fallout cloud pass.

OUTLOOK CROONING

Got no world on a string.
Nor make the rain go.

I'm in Napa, she says.
A woman in a plaid pink hat.

We're all in a kind of Napa.

And the little marks
around my eyes. Finicky marks.

Nothing rapt.

For example, some get off
watching women clean windows.

Many things might have been beautiful.

A motel swimming pool.
A woman in a plaid hat drinking Coors.

Vague skies. Fingertips
pressed to glass.

Simple that.

Shouldn't boohoo. Got no ocean
in my nose. No dawning idea.

But clothes, California. Suppose

I worked spotting fires in
some forested nowhere. All day
through the scope with my Over. Charlie. Over.

Suppose such a lofted thing. Corrugated. Serene.
Distant tufts of smoke.

Shouldn't even sing.

AND WHY NOT JUST KAMIKAZE

for Robert

Some of us
live in parking lots, bleary
and incoherent from
meth, awake only
in a remembered middle
school, painting houses when
we're sober. *Paging*
Vincent Guerra. Vincent Guerra
to the principal's office. Remember
when you laid the wreath
at Arlington? Remember when we
slept side by side in sleeping
bags on my bedroom floor? This
is how God
blesses us, a good
heart. All else
is Caesar's.

SOMETHING'S COMING SOON

Someone hung clay faces
on the tree trunks for the children.
Maybe the children themselves.

Most things I won't even mention.
The Italian family eating omelets by the window.
Would it matter if they were German?

Today the sky is both inspiration
and expiration, both somber
and searing heaven.

I am my own mother reciting stories to ease me.
I lie on my back on the wooden floor,
and in another room the faucet starts.

What do I really need, anyway?
I shrug at what comes.

It runs clear in me.

The color washes out

of the strip malls, new mattresses,
future realms of matter.

Washes out
of the highway and the trees.

Lights come on
and, through the night,

stay with us.

THE YEAR I FINALLY FAKE MY DEATH

I could run now and be gone,
abandon my plans of stardom.

The manzanitas
in the headlights are ghosts
on the backs of dimes.

The way home is a foreign country.

And the amber bottle slides back
in the corrugated bed
but doesn't break.

Where are we going
that we'd wreck
just to watch an empty glass

become useless.

I've traded all my coins
for plastic coins,

and I don't know if anyone will welcome me.

But I'm in my dream head,

and the faces in the cars
that slow behind our pickup
stare back through the glass.

My hands are my same
child hands.

It doesn't matter where we're headed.

DEAD MAN

New Year's with Reactive Arthritis

Doxycycline's
Tiffany-blue poison

early '90s pop songs

      fireworks   farther down the beach, fizzling

into the surf   The stars
were a mess

I didn't know what

      I should have been doing

so I sang
the songs I knew

and hid my face
      in a red solo cup

of five-dollar champagne

      The couples swaddled

and the beach shushed
      as they kissed and whispered

*

I tried to read ahead

     the uncanny patterns
of illness

I didn't know then

     I'd meet you in a blizzard

three months later

What I felt
     I believed

as myopic as Missouri

     What is now always shall be

The way, as kids
     we'd ignore a salt and pepper storm

on the TV, most days
     I could still see
my life through the pain

a faint life

*

And in the New Year morning   everything shines

tree limbs
parked cars

thin waves shine
like pavement

a chair left out on the deck
Monterey pines
sand and
my arms, my hands

*

Like I said, there were two storms

one with real snow

an overcrowded room
where I spent fifteen minutes with you

which was enough

You wore a red coat
We split an orange

When I left I thought

dragging my suitcase through the slush

I'd never see you again

Still, I hefted that suitcase
            on ruined legs
            through a blizzard
            toward a life I didn't want

relieved that you existed

The Manatees

scud
through cone-spur,
    baby's tears, common
    waterweed; their bodies a kind of punishment, seized
        in concrete. Algae, light chains
      of spittle between surface and estuary
       floor, fix their incompatible world
    to ours, a world as foreign
as the ornate levels of hell and crowded
   afterlives of fifteenth-century Italian frescos.
The sacrificial organs, castoffs
     of the tide's weird laboratory, coil in shallows by roadside
       grass and foreclosed condos, and in the chambers
   of Fra Angelico's *Last Judgment*, the naked
      console each other
   as they're mutilated and devoured by b-movie
monsters. Even as a child, I knew
   to step into lake water was to allow oneself
to be ingested, but I've often mistaken
   what's terrified me.
                  So, the joints arrest. So,
  the immune system mutinies. The music leaves.
    The mind endlessly replicates
the worst outcome, and when I couldn't
   walk anymore
it seemed I had been forever

cast from the beautiful ease of my body
into the forlorn, cartoonish
overcoat of the manatee, my final summons
into the menagerie, as one of the waggish
creatures of our queer world.

Am I paralyzed?

I am so still. There's no one
to check.

I don't have it in me
to check again. That, right there,

that disobedient wrist
confirms it. Let the thrashing

commence. Why can't I glimmer
like a ginger dog

who's squandered
its past life as a medieval

peasant? Why can't I
wear ribbons? Or these old

ruminations: is it the same

sock if darned of all
its thread, as we are darned

of every cell
after so many years, which

is nature, over and over,
forgiving us?

But the strands that remember
our first selves

clone their own frailty
till we resemble gaunt furniture

made of driftwood
sold alongside the road. We will

be passed by
cars and partake

of their brief and muffled music.

Discarded Cosmos

I tallied the wayward objects: a clustered galaxy
   of cellophane marooned in grass, a napkin
      crumpled to coral, a drinking straw's shucked cocoon
   flattened on the path. Whose lips these things
      have touched and where and why? Whose hands
undid them? Where do the clothes on the forest floor
      come from? I know a man who squirrels
   cardboard coffee sleeves
            in his coat pockets. He knows the value
   of each thing. I learn an elderly
      pace from the woman gazing through
         the parking lot's chain-link
   at the highway and fast-
food joints, from the man in reflective tape
      nightly beneath the Spanish moss
apparitioned in my headlights—these pioneers
         of routine. Someday
   no one will pay attention to me, too, and I can be odd
      and unreliable. In front of me at K-Mart,
   an old man places smoke alarms, a wall clock,
         toilet plunger, a small flashlight, large
flashlight, rodent traps, and ant traps on the conveyor—
   he is moving into
      a new apartment. He hunches out of breath
   on the counter. The backs of his hands
are blue; he is going to die, probably,

within the year. Still,
there is new breath
in this constellation of things, an effervescence,
a delicate life.

HABERDASHERY

When we are young, our clothing
is colorful. Thereafter, we gradually
drab, until we are old and bloom
again. We reclaim
the wispy hair of children.
Like that old woman
in a wheelchair hunched
over her ice cream cone
in a dandelion dress—she
is not one of those thin raincoat wearers.
But the men
take a little wilderness with them
in their hats, a little foliage. Who
among us can wear
yellow shoes but a toddling elder?
Beneath a tree, a Van Gogh
cherry blossom. A nineteenth-century
blue sky. The adolescents
smoking in the doorways,
they, too, feel the thaw
and pliant summering taking place—
even with our criminally
unjust tax code! They're not

going to kill themselves
today. They'll huddle inside
for coffee, their tense and perfect
bodies beneath overpasses of coats.

Rewrite

Farewell to spring   phantom
orchid

fire crews in white shirts
eat barbecue

along highway 70—

it's summertime   expect the wildfire

in Quincy   a canyon blaze in Colfax
but the meadows

of the wrists—cream cups
fiddlenecks   lark-

spur   spreading

flox   all the slash   underbrush
dazzle   the ankles

crammed with gravel   shoulders just snag—
I couldn't

walk and didn't
know why   I couldn't

climb the lookout—only the close
smoke   oak lungfuls

over the Auburn hills   blankets

soaked by faulty
ziplock bags of ice

while my joints   little hot spots
reduced me

to months in bed
with junk TV

waking up
in flames   my entire arm

tinder
or not sleep at all   I couldn't

straighten my legs

      *

Goodbye   glassy onion   goodbye
wild rye   the birr

of being twenty-nine   Life
I told myself

would not be the same
that charm

warped to cinereal
char

and a line from Walser
warned me

One's always waiting
for something   well   that tends
to weaken one

Illness burnt all I waited for
away

in that germinating furnace   the manzanitas
rewrote themselves

into the leafmeal

Dead Man

One cannot respond to phantoms. Nor fish-startle. Phantom shadow. Phantom mother's call. One must let oneself drift beyond the yellow rope. Beyond the bobbers and buoy. One must leave oneself alone. As one's been left alone. One must raise some concern. Disown another breath. Diminish the heart. Let the legs wilt through numb realms. Into a green corridor of submerged light. One can't be afraid of losing friends. One must be dead to friends. Dead Man through Sharks and Fishes. Dead Man through Marco Polo. One must be dead to float at all. And if no one calls. And if no one notices the boy face-down a distance from the others. One must convince them. One must persist. One can't rescue oneself. Still the breath runs out. And the jig is up. The paralyzed jig. The overwrought performance. Still better than lying on a towel being looked at by people. Better than burning one's skin to shit. And the shittiness of one's sister. Better than this crowded ambivalence. Some entire days are Dead Mans. Of gazing at the lake's dumb floor. And the done-in grip on the buoy. And one's cheek against a warm, dropleted arm. The eased breath of this. Without the pressure on the lungs. And if one looks back for distance-muffled applause. As one should not. From some toddler or someone else's mother. And one figures no one's noticed at all. And all have done their best in their own performance. One can swim, finally, back to shore. We all can be forgiven.

Acknowledgments

Grateful thanks to the following publications, in which versions of these poems first appeared: *Anti-, Barrow Street, Bat City Review, Boston Review, Cincinnati Review, Crazyhorse, Denver Quarterly, Everyday Genius, Field, Indiana Review, Meridian, Narrative Magazine, The Southern Review,* and *Washington Square Review.*

Vincent Guerra grew up in northern California and received an MFA from Washington University in St. Louis and a PhD from Florida State University. He currently resides in Boston, MA.

Publication of this book was made possible by grants and donations. We are also grateful to those individuals who participated in our 2016 Build a Book Program. They are:

Anonymous (8), Evan Archer, Sally Ball, Jan Bender-Zanoni, Zeke Berman, Kristina Bicher, Carol Blum, Lee Briccetti, Deirdre Brill, Anthony Cappo, Carla & Steven Carlson, Maxwell Dana, Machi Davis, Monica Ferrell, Martha Webster & Robert Fuentes, Dorothy Goldman, Lauri Grossman, Steven Haas, Mary Heilner, Henry Israeli, Christopher Kempf, David Lee, Jen Levitt, Howard Levy, Owen Lewis, Paul Lisicky, Katie Longofono, Cynthia Lowen, Louise Mathias, Nathan McClain, Gregory McDonald, Britt Melewski, Kamilah Aisha Moon, Carolyn Murdoch, Tracey Orick, Zachary Pace, Gregory Pardlo, Allyson Paty, Marcia & Chris Pelletiere, Eileen Pollack, Barbara Preminger, Kevin Prufer, Peter & Jill Schireson, Roni & Richard Schotter, Soraya Shalforoosh, Peggy Shinner, James Snyder & Krista Fragos, Megan Staffel, Marjorie & Lew Tesser, Susan Walton, Calvin Wei, Abigail Wender, Allison Benis White, and Monica Youn.